NOT ALWAYS
ALL TOGETHER
KATHERINE WALDEN

To my family in Christ, with whom I have the privilege of doing life with. For better or worse, through laughter and tears, we make up the Body of Christ.

Table of Contents

Not Always
All Together

WHAT OTHERS ARE SAYING

"**Not Always All Together**" by Katherine Walden is a devotional recipe for finding beauty and growth in the mess of life. Katherine weaves a mix of life stories with the application of God's word. Through her own transparency, humour, (and a tasty bean casserole recipe), she comforts, delights, and challenges the reader to a new perspective. Katherine doesn't let her reader get away with admiring jewels of spiritual wisdom. No, she sets you up, for breakthrough!

Sue Carpenter - *Carpenter's Cross Ministries*

Katherine's writings help you come into a deeper place of intimacy with God, help you love yourself, and show the true treasure of the Kingdom. As Katherine writes, she is a vessel for Holy Spirit, and what you read is His heart. I have to confess that sometimes I'm too busy to hear what He is saying, and too focused on myself to see His majesty. These devotionals help me see what I'm missing.

Dennis Wood - *Twice Blessed Ministries*

"**Not Always All Together**," Katherine's third devotional, is her best yet. Her honest and vulnerable stories taken from a lifetime of serving God will first disarm you and then hit you right between the eyes with truths that have to be acted on. This is not a book you can read quickly unless your heart is locked away so much it can't be touched. These devotionals are to be savoured, meditated on, and lived out in the world so their truth can permeate your life and lead you deeper into Christ.

John Spencer - *Author of "The Lost Parables" series*

If you enjoy new adventures in life and yet you are also comforted by what is common to us all, then "**Not Always All Together**" is definitely a devotional that will bless your heart. Katherine takes us on an adventure, weaving the common threads and surprises that touch our lives each and every day. A refreshing new twist to an age-old message: God loves us and He sees us in our daily walk with Him. This devotional is both challenging and comforting. I highly recommend it.

Julie Smude - *YWAM Thailand*

I love this little book of short stories (devotionals) and the corresponding scriptures Katherine includes! Each one challenges me to draw closer to God and encourages me to live my life in a way that would be beneficial to those around me. And not just my children and friends but also the strangers I might meet in my daily travels. Her "lessons" fill me with hope and inspire me to make a difference, even while I'm still on my own journey and even before I get it "all together."

Howard Henig - *Redding, CA*

PREFACE

My home is the very model of a peaceful and harmonious abode. Rarely is a harsh word spoken and petty jealousies do not exist. There is never a problem with someone taking too long in the shower. The toilet seat is always in the right position, and there are never any arguments over the TV remote. No one complains that the music is too loud, too old-fashioned, or too boring.

You'd be hard pressed to hear testy words or sarcastic comebacks; baleful glares and slammed doors are rarely witnessed. Household birthdays and anniversaries are never forgotten. Temper tantrums are never thrown. The trash is taken out without complaint or the need of a reminder. There has never been a disagreement about financial planning, and all purchase decisions are met with unanimous approval.

Before you protest that such a domestic utopia could never exist, perhaps I should mention one important fact. I live alone. I don't claim any moral or spiritual superiority to the rest of the world. Living alone leaves me vulnerable to leading a self-centred lifestyle. If it were not for my brothers and sisters in Christ and the people I meet in my daily life, I'd be doomed to live a miserable existence of self-delusion. Fortunately for me, I am given many opportunities to see the actual condition of my heart on a regular basis.

God uses the weaknesses and strengths of my brothers and sisters in Christ to shed light on my own strengths and weaknesses. He allows others to rub me the wrong way in the hope that my garments of self-righteousness and self-defensiveness are worn so thin that I finally discard them. My world-wide spiritual family comes alongside me, lending me their strength when I am weak and close to stumbling. I bolster their faith when they are down. We might disagree at times and see life challenges from different doctrinal positions, but in the end, we all agree that without Jesus as our head, we would fall into disunity and strife. We love each other enough to speak the truth in love if need be and we are there to bring comfort and hope to one another when disaster hits. No, the body of Christ doesn't always work like a well-oiled machine, but I am forever grateful that He planted me in this loving, caring, and sometimes dysfunctional family.

I have included a personal application with each of the 31 devotions contained in this book. I encourage you to take the time to answer the question prompts and then meditate on the scriptures and inspirational quotes provided. Go through the book with a group of friends as it will not only deepen your commitment one to another. It is my sincere hope that this little book will bring healing and restoration to those who have been wounded in the church.

I also created YouTube videos that are well under 5 minutes each that provide additional content not found in the book. You can find those free videos on my YouTube channel, look for Katherine Walden Ministries and you'll find them there. Feel free to comment on the videos and I will be sure to respond!

Our Heavenly Father created us to do life within His family. He invites the *'not always all together'* to come together to do His will on the Earth. So let's begin!

Psalm 133 (NLT)

"How wonderful and pleasant it is
when brothers live together in harmony!
For harmony is as precious as the anointing oil
that was poured over Aaron's head,
that ran down his beard
and onto the border of his robe.
Harmony is as refreshing as the dew from Mount Hermon
that falls on the mountains of Zion.
And there the Lord has pronounced his blessing,
even life everlasting."

Not Always All Together

Lunch with the Family

Acts 2: 46-47 — "And day by day, attending the temple together and breaking bread in their homes, they received their food with glad and generous hearts, praising God and having favour with all the people. And the Lord added to their number day by day those who were being saved."

I toyed with my omelette, interested more in the conversation around the table than by my meal. John masterfully wove stories of faith and of God's provision. Even as we laughed at John's slightly self-derisive humour, I could see that his stories of provision touched the heart of one of our companions who was in the middle of a financial crisis. At one point John paused, then looked me straight in the eye as we sat in a moment of silence. I am sure you know that look, the look that searches the motivations of your heart. I learned later through a mutual friend that I passed inspection.

As the conversations started back up and I watched fellowship in action, I couldn't help but remember a lunch I shared with other believers as a very young Christian. On that day, my companions and I ate off metal dishes. The fare was cafeteria food at its worst, and the ambience was as unappealing as the grey mashed potatoes on my plate. I sat quietly that day, observing my new friends as they talked.

I could sense pain behind their easy banter and boisterous ribbing. Their life experiences were wedged in every line on their faces. At the same time, I discerned a depth in their Christian walk that I frankly envied. Their arms bore many tattoos, the occasional cuss word shot out here and there, but there was a fellowship of the heart around the table as brothers and sisters broke bread, all one family in Christ.

Our luncheon's locale was the guest area of a high-risk, medium-security prison. My lunch mates were admitted murderers, drug pushers, and violent offenders. I am sure if my mother had known where I was going that day, she would have had a justifiable heart attack. In the natural, a men's prison was no place for a 19-year-old girl.

My duties that day were simple; carry the songbooks and Bibles we brought with us, and chat with the inmates. I was a young Christian, practically a baby, and many of the men I dined with had walked with the Lord for decades. I confess that I failed in one of my tasks as I found myself listening to their counsel and speaking little. I knew I didn't have much to offer beyond my presence, and I sensed these brothers in Christ had much to teach me.

I saw no difference between these men and myself. Several of them had backgrounds remarkably like my own. Without Christ's intervention, I probably would have followed the same path that led to their incarceration. Their heart-level understanding of God's unconditional forgiveness and love, their willingness to take responsibility for their crimes, and their decision to change their lives for the better with Christ's help inspired me.

Thirty years later, as I chatted with my new friend, John, our conversation drifted to prison food. He struggled most of his life with addictions and as a result ended up on the wrong side of the law more than once. We laughed and swapped stories, and I silently thanked God for the lessons that I learned in that prison cafeteria so long ago. Although John's life journey has not allowed us to cross paths very often, I count him as a friend, and I believe he sees me as a sister in Christ.

Personal Application

In my story, I mentioned that I learned from the men in the prison by focusing on them and listening to their stories.

How well do you listen? It takes practice to be a good listener but it is a skill worth developing.

Here are some tips that might be of help to you as you seek to be a better listener:

1. Shift your body so you are facing the speaker.

2. Keep natural eye contact.

3. Put away your phone, turn off your computer, limit distractions.

4. Respond appropriately to show that you understand. Use both verbal and body language cues to show you are listening. Nod and smile. Wait for natural pauses in the conversation to ask questions. Ask questions that help them to continue their story. "Then what did you do?" and "How did you feel?"

5. Focus on what the speaker is saying. Don't try to think out your response.

6. If you find your mind wandering, tell yourself to pay attention. It works!

7. Wait until the speaker completes their thought before you assume you know where their story is going.

8. Give feedback and don't be afraid to ask questions for clarification.

9. Paraphrase what you think they said, and speak it in response. "I am not sure, but I believe you are saying…"

IT PROBABLY DOESN'T MAKE MUCH SENSE

On a breezy spring day, I welcomed the warmth of the sunlight streaming through huge skylights in a sprawling hospital as I made my way through the mazes of corridors and elevators. As I rounded the last corner, welcoming smiles greeted me. I parked my scooter in a niche and settled into a more comfortable chair in the waiting room of an intensive care unit.

The Lord gathered us together that day. We were a small band of believers, but we served a big God. We placed our trust in Him as we began to pray. Experts had told the family that the medical situation was impossible. They gave us little hope in the past - and God defied their prognosis. As we pressed on in prayer, our faith rested on God's Word and our weary hearts found comfort in a real sense of His presence.

After an hour or two of prayer, I made my way home. Thinking back on my afternoon, I laughed softly. How foolish our prayer group might have appeared to unbelievers when they walked past us. What a band of mighty warriors indeed! I arrived in a scooter for the disabled. Next to me sat a brother in Christ who lived with an inflammatory disease that stiffened every joint in his body, twisted his hands and feet, and left him in chronic pain. To his right, sat a woman who was a cancer survivor. To her right, sat a sweet sister in Christ whose heart condition required rest and a stringent diet.

I marvelled at God's ways; He brought this group together, weak in body, but strong in spirit. Our assignment; to pray. That afternoon, the medical crisis was averted.

God uses the weak to demonstrate His power. He does so to drive the point home; it is only through Him that the miraculous is performed. It is not by our might, nor by our power. (Zechariah 4:6) He partners with the weak by leading them to impossible places, then works through them to bring about breakthrough. God does so to encourage His children and broadcast His loving heart to a lost creation.

1 Corinthians 1:25-31 – For the foolishness of God is wiser than men, and the weakness of God is stronger than men. For consider your calling, brothers: not many of you were wise according to worldly standards, not many were powerful, not many were of noble birth. But God chose what is foolish in the world to shame the wise; God chose what is weak in the world to shame the strong; God chose what is low and despised in the world, even things that are not, to bring to nothing things that are, so that no human being might boast in the presence of God. And because of him you are in Christ Jesus, who became to us wisdom from God, righteousness and sanctification and redemption, so that, as it is written, "Let the one who boasts, boast in the Lord."

Personal Application

Think back on a critical point in your life where without the support of others, you would have never made your way through to the other side. Give thanks for that band of friends!

Do you believe that weakness disqualifies you from being used by God? Many of the heroes of our faith suffered with one form of disability or another. Moses believed he was a poor orator, Paul had weak eyesight, Timothy had a stomach ailment. Elijah was prone to long episodes of depression. Read biographies of the early pioneers of the modern missionary movement, and you will discover many of them suffered with some form of chronic disability or physical weakness BEFORE they left for the mission field. Many of these heroes answered God's call even as they wondered why He would call them, when so many were better equipped than themselves.

What would you do today if you honestly believed that God uses the weak to bring glory to Himself?

Not Always All Together

GOD'S SANCTIONED SPENDING SPREE

I am thankful for the financial lessons I learned during my missionary years. I didn't have an infinite stream of funds in my bank account then, and I now live on a fixed disability pension. God abundantly supplies for my needs, but He doesn't indulge my every whim. It is my practice to set aside money each month for yearly personal expenditures, such as insurance. I try to set aside funds for the upkeep of my ministry's websites, hosting fees, and the like.

When donations are down, and ministry expenses skyrocket, it is tempting to use my credit card. After all, I have an excellent credit rating! Why not get that software package that would make my life easier? Why not hire an editor to edit my next book? Why shouldn't I use a line of credit to travel to another city for a conference that would enhance my ministry's effectiveness while providing much-needed personal refreshment? The simple answer is; it is not good stewardship to go into debt. My transitory wants, wishes, and whims must give way to mundane necessities. I don't have an unlimited supply of cash.

It is particularly tempting to dip into designated funds when I see the opportunity to bless another person. I love giving. I know intercessory prayer is a powerful gift to spend on behalf of someone else. However, I find it deeply satisfying when I can place a gift in a friend's hands as a tangible reminder of God's great love for them. I pout when my ability to bless others is thwarted by my lack of funds.

Fortunately, I can spend the currency of God's kingdom with no thought of His funds running dry. In fact, God encourages me to spend this currency even if I think there is nothing left in my stores. Sometimes, He asks me to use much more than I want to spend. After all, He reasons, with such a constant stream of resources, there is no need to set aside a portion for later use. A rainy-day fund is not necessary. God assures me that if I invest His currency into all those I meet today, I will have more than enough for those who might have a greater need tomorrow.

What is His currency? Love.

I discovered the more I pour out love, the more God pours love into my storehouse.

Personal Application

Think about the last statement, "I discovered the more I pour out love, the more God pours love into my storehouse."

Are you afraid that loving freely will give people an open invitation to take advantage of you? Have you been betrayed in the past? Is it a pattern in your life? You hold the power to break that pattern. Today is a new day!

On a blank sheet of paper, make a list of each person who took advantage of you. Forgive them and release them from any emotional debt you feel they owe you. Forgiveness will allow you to move on.

Learn to set loving and honouring boundaries.

I highly recommend the following two books. Both these authors have free materials on the Internet as well.

Cloud, Henry, and John Sims Townsend. *Boundaries: When to Say Yes, How to Say No to Take Control of Your Life*. Grand Rapids, Mich: Zondervan, 2012. Print and Kindle. Workbooks are available.

Silk, Danny. *Keep Your Love On!: Connection, Communication & Boundaries*. United States: Loving on Purpose, 2015. Print and Kindle. Teaching materials are available on Danny's website.

TRAVEL LIGHT

One of the first lessons you learn in Youth With A Mission (YWAM) is "Keep your possessions few."

When I first joined YWAM, I expected to be gone from home for about five months. I left with two huge suitcases as well as a sleeping bag and a pillow. I flew from Calgary to Toronto, then travelled by bus to a small town about two hours north of Toronto, all in the same day. In Calgary, my family helped me check my bags. Once I landed in Toronto though, I was on my own. My aunt offered to pick me up at the Toronto airport and drive me to the bus station, but she was unable to lift more than a few pounds. As I dragged my belongings across the large airport terminal, I wondered, "Do I honestly need all this stuff?" Hauling my possessions to the bus was no less of a struggle.

Late that night, when I finally arrived at my destination, I was stiff, sore, and frustrated. That frustration grew into distress when I was ushered into a 13 by 13 square foot room that I would be sharing with five other girls. There were no dressers and no closets. The room was empty except for three utilitarian bunk beds.

What to do with all my junk? Much of it landed in a crawl space until the end of the training portion of my mission school. Leadership informed us that each team member would be limited to a small suitcase, sleeping bag and pillow on our two-month outreach. We would be travelling through several climates. As I sorted through my belongings, it became apparent that I had used only twenty percent of what I brought with me. Most of my possessions were left behind, shoved into a dark, dusty storage room.

The next year, I travelled from Ontario to Hawaii for further ministry opportunities. I wasn't sure if I'd be returning, so everything I owned went with me. I travelled to Texas on a crowded school bus with thirty-two adults and five children. I then flew to California and spent a week there before flying on to Hawaii. A small car pulled up outside the airport to greet me and three other YWAMers. We travelled a considerable distance to a remote part of the island, and most of us carried luggage on our laps.

As I hauled my now battered suitcases up a steep set of stairs, I began to grasp the wisdom of the 'less is more' theory. And when I entered a cavernous room full of bunk beds with no storage, I was ready to baptise my suitcases in the nearby ocean!

Several weeks after my arrival in Hawaii, we were given a challenge. As the mission base was in a financial crunch, our leadership felt we were to practise generosity amongst ourselves, as a community. As a result, we would see a breakthrough in our corporate finances.

As I asked the Lord what I should give, I rifled through my luggage. I found a dual alarm clock radio that I hadn't used in almost two years. I set it aside, along with half my clothing. The clothes landed in the base's clothing exchange room, but not before I washed them thoroughly. They were beyond musty!

I felt led to give the clock radio to a young couple. I didn't know why I was to provide them with that clock, but I felt it was to go to them! When I arrived at their door with my gift in hand, they broke into tears. Their clock had stopped working earlier that day. They specifically needed a dual alarm as the husband had a part-time job and needed to awaken two hours earlier than his wife. They prayed that morning but did not tell anyone of their need. Within hours – that need was met. As a bonus, my baggage became much lighter.

Personal Application

If you are feeling frustrated, crowded and disorganised in your home, ask yourself a simple question. "Is there too much clutter in my life?" Do you have a closet full of closed and sealed boxes that have been untouched for years? Start to give away or sell any item you have not used or displayed in the past two years. You will immediately notice clarity, freedom, and openness!

We can also be cluttered in our spirits. Ask yourself, "Do I have a closet in my spirit with sealed boxes full of gifts, insights, and lessons that I haven't accessed in years?" If so, share those treasures! Use them to bless others.

IMAGINE STEPPING OUT

Charlene Dyer is a good friend of mine and I had the joy and privilege of walking beside her as she courageously stepped out of isolation and back into Christian community. Several years ago, she gave me permission to share a poem she wrote from the perspective of someone whom society often marginalises.

Charlene is now a member of a great church and is surrounded by people who cheer her on as she continues her remarkable journey of restoration. She has determined to remain faithful in her walk despite increasingly challenging obstacles. Her quiet example influences many in her growing circle of friends as they press on for breakthroughs in their own lives. Many of those friends are people that many might choose to ignore.

Imagine

Imagine believing you deserve to be treated with dignity.
Imagine believing you deserve the touch of a tender hand, a tender hug.
A person does not have to earn love, can you imagine?

Imagine standing up for yourself, some will hate it,

but imagine gaining confidence!

Imagine people offering their friendship and not asking for anything

in return.

Peace of mind, we all deserve.

We all deserve to be pulled up when we fall, without judgment

We all deserve freedom to stand on solid ground

Freedom to be you, the "you" God made you to be

Freedom to be happy and peaceful, to have someone proud of you.

Let's stand strong

Let's teach the people in our lives

that we all deserve goodness, love, and respect.

Take the time to notice the lonely,

the sick and the forgotten

Step out of your comfort zone

Treat people as equals

Teach that we are all special.

Give the scared and the abused ones

lots of patience and love.

They deserve it.

Offer them your hand

but don't take it personally if they stand back.

Offer them the kind of love and patience God gives us.

Let them see the Light in our eyes.

God wants all of us to have His love and patience,

we never need to earn it.

Imagine that!

———————

Personal Application

As you read Charlene's poem, did anyone come to mind? Don't take them on as a personal project. No one deserves to be dehumanised by becoming a do-gooder's endeavour. Buy them a coffee, make it point to acknowledge that you see them with a casual smile or nod. Reach out in friendship. More than likely, you will learn more from them than they will learn from you.

NEVER MIND, I'LL DO IT MYSELF

A child's aspiration to help others is a key marker of emotional health and development. A wise caregiver looks for opportunities to encourage a child in this area of growth. Quite often, these opportunities present themselves at the precise time when it would be more convenient for an adult to do the task.

It would be easier for a parent of a new-born to dash upstairs to grab a diaper than to ask a preschool sibling to fetch that diaper. However, a wise parent knows that sibling rivalry and jealousy can be curbed by including the older child in age-appropriate caregiving tasks. Not only does this encourage the older sibling to become more independent, but it also helps that child see that they can make a difference in another person's life.

Parents who look for opportunities of service for their child expand that child's horizons, nurture their self-worth and open their eyes to see the needs of others. The time invested in allowing their toddler to stumble through their little tasks will pay big dividends later in life.

Similarly, one marker of a Christian's growth is their desire to serve others. When combined with the realisation that they can make a positive difference in the lives of those around them through acts of service, real growth takes place. A wise leader looks for opportunities to encourage new believers in this area.

Christ demonstrated this principle by sending His disciples to do His works. It would have been easier for Him to go and heal the sick, deliver those in bondage, raise the dead, and proclaim the good news by Himself. He sent His disciples with the knowledge that in their human frailty, they would make a mess of things more than once. However, Jesus never once said to His disciples. "Never mind, I'll do it myself."

Although there is a risk involved, we must allow new believers to grow in faith by ministering one to another. To deny them this opportunity will stunt their growth and discourage them from doing the things of Christ.

A dear friend of mine finally chose to be baptised after struggling with the lie that she must be spiritually mature before she could be considered a worthy candidate for baptism. Through prayer, counsel, and faith, she chose to walk past that false belief and embrace the truth. Her expression of joy in finding freedom brought those who witnessed her baptism to tears.

The fruits of her encounter with God in the baptismal waters were made clear soon after by her acts of service. It was the custom in our church to pray for one another. "Everyone gets to play" as John Wimber once said. For several years prior, my friend received much prayer and encouragement, but in those years, she did not feel comfortable praying for others as she felt she had nothing to offer. On the Sunday following her baptism, my friend prayed for several of her friends.

Although there were more seasoned prayer warriors in the congregation that day, God spoke to her heart. He asked her to take baby steps. The more experienced in the church that day did not step in. After all, she had received plenty of teaching about prayer, and she had observed the prayer team in action for years. No one pushed her aside in their desire to help. Instead, they joined their prayers with hers as they observed from afar, trusting Christ in her, the hope of glory. (Col 1:27)

If you find it hard to resist doing it all by yourself because you believe you can do a better job than anyone else, may I remind you of the wisdom displayed by the leaders of the early church? The apostles realised they could not do it all. They relinquished control of certain aspects of their ministry to those they trained and released. Those to whom they assigned simple tasks went on to be used mightily by God.

Acts 6:2b-4 — "It is not right that we should give up preaching the word of God to serve tables. Therefore, brothers, pick out from among you seven men of good repute, full of the Spirit and of wisdom, whom we will appoint to this duty. But we will devote ourselves to prayer and to the ministry of the word."

By permitting other disciples of Jesus to minister to the body, the Apostles allowed the Church to expand and grow. If you find those whom you lead and mentor becoming stagnant in their faith, look for opportunities that will enable them to grow through service.

Personal Application

Are you a delegator or are you a 'never mind, I'll do it myself' sort of person? What are the drawbacks of each? What are the pluses?

If you are a leader or a parent, set those under you up for success. Give them both the tools and the space they need to do the job assigned. Make sure your instructions are clear. State the expected results of the tasks you set before them. Give positive feedback and create an atmosphere where questions are encouraged.

Jesus led by example. He showed His disciples how to heal the sick and cast out demons. The Master sent His disciples out to do what He taught them. He didn't micromanage. He didn't even go along on their ministry trips to make sure they were doing what He asked them to do.

If loved ones or employees have confronted you about your controlling tendencies, spend some time with the Lord. Identify the underlying fear that causes you to keep a tight rein on your family and those you lead.

Does the Attire Make a Christian?

In the late seventies, I attended a church that had a specific dress code. It quickly became apparent to newcomers that Sunday-evening service attendance required formal suits for men and long gowns or skirts for women. Perfectly coifed hair and expertly applied makeup were a necessity. In the morning services, sports jackets and ties for men and dresses or skirts for women were expected. I was living on a junior office worker's salary, and my wardrobe was not as extensive as many in the congregation. I bought my clothes at Sears; whereas many of the women shopped in high-end boutiques. I rotated between my formal graduation dress and a bridesmaid dress on Sunday nights.

My Sunday morning attire was nearly as limited. My everyday wardrobe consisted of jeans, T-shirts, work slacks, casual sweaters, and the occasional button-down blouse. My makeup routine consisted of blush, lip gloss, and a hint of mascara. Although many women in the church wore their hair in elaborate styles, I wore my hair long and straight. Walking into the church was like visiting a foreign country. My friends and I stood out for all the wrong reasons.

I loved my church, and I am grateful for the foundational truths I received as a new believer. Week after week, my friends and I would eagerly climb out of my brother's beaten-up old car, making sure not to scratch the Cadillacs parked next to us. Yes, we were hungry for the word, but we desperately needed mentorship and discipling. Fortunately for us, one couple saw past our less-than-perfect attire and saw our hunger. They invited us into their home for a weekly Bible study.

Once they realised their newfound friends were singles who lived on their own, Harley and Pat changed their schedule to include a weekly potluck. The teachings we received were practical and life-affirming. Harley was a successful entrepreneur and took us through Biblical money-management strategies. Pat quickly became our older sister. She taught us how to be gracious hosts and hostesses and showed us how to wear our faith on our sleeve through Christ-like attitudes and unconditional love. In turn, we brought a fresh perspective to Pat and Harley. As they were immersed in church for many years, they had lost touch with the culture outside the church walls. We reassured them that it was all right to let their hair down occasionally.

Since then, I have fellowshipped with believers in many nations. I joined in the congregational singing of "How Great Thou Art" while sitting on the dirt floor of a bamboo hut in a third-world country, and I sang the same song while sitting on a nicely padded pew.

I currently attend a church where most people dress casually. One of our pastors regularly preaches in shorts in the summer; whereas our former pastor, who has now gone on to be with the Lord, preferred comfortable sweaters and jeans. Women wear slacks or jeans unless the heat of a summer day dictates that a skirt, modest shorts or a sundress would be more appropriate, given the lack of air conditioning in the gym we rent.

Several members of our congregation are refugees from African nations. It is the standard within their cultures to dress in their Sunday-best, colourful dresses for the women, suits for the men. Their younger daughters wear frilly dresses and bows while their younger sons sport dress shirts. Our casual attire took them off guard at first. Some wondered why Canadians couldn't afford to dress better.

Our African brothers and sisters fled their homelands, arriving in our nation with little more than their faith. Their passion for Jesus is infectious, and they pray with the authority that only comes through victories won by years of faithful endurance during severe persecution. While the colourful attire of my African brothers and sisters bring a vibrant accent to the jeans and T-shirts the rest of our congregation wear, their spiritual attire brings accents of eternal value: life, joy, and wisdom.

Our generous God provides us with the garments of salvation and righteousness. May we wear these garments with dignity, grace, and vulnerability.

Isaiah 61:10 — "I will greatly rejoice in the Lord; my soul shall exult in my God, for he has clothed me with the garments of salvation; he has covered me with the robe of righteousness, as a bridegroom decks himself like a priest with a beautiful headdress, and as a bride adorns herself with her jewels."

Personal Application

1 Corinthians 9:19-23 MSG – "Even though I am free of the demands and expectations of everyone, I have voluntarily become a servant to any and all in order to reach a wide range of people: religious, nonreligious, meticulous moralists, loose-living immoralists, the defeated, the demoralised—whoever. I didn't take on their way of life. I kept my bearings in Christ—but I entered their world and tried to experience things from their point of view. I've become just about every sort of servant there is in my attempts to lead those I meet into a God-saved life. I did all this because of the Message. I didn't just want to talk about it; I wanted to be in on it!"

While Paul refused to renounce the tenets of his faith, he wasn't afraid to immerse himself in the everyday life and culture of whatever town or region the Lord led him. Paul didn't expect people to conform to his way of life, but he did lead them to the Way and the Life.

How welcome are the seekers, the curious, and the newly saved in your faith community? Would they feel like a fish out of water if they were to walk into your sanctuary wearing casual yet modest attire? Are there certain unspoken dress codes in your church that present a stumbling block to those who cannot afford to dress a certain way? Are those principles based on Christian foundational doctrine or are they based on your denominational culture?

Are there younger people in your congregation or faith community who aren't plugged in? Try to reach out to them, take them out for coffee after church one Sunday! Ask questions, listen to their needs, and then seek the Lord as to how you can help meet those needs.

Cultivate a Teachable Heart

Have you ever watched children as they take in information through all their senses? Their faces light up as they discover the wonder of something new. Their little bodies twitch with excitement at the thought of new discoveries lurking right around the corner. A good teacher knows how to capture a child's imagination; an extraordinarily gifted teacher knows how to draw out child-like inquisitiveness in their audience.

Jesus was the greatest teacher of all. He captured the minds, imaginations, and hearts of those who chose to humble themselves and open their hearts to his truth. Jesus used numerous methods in his teaching style. He told parables, he gave object lessons, and he called his disciples' attention to the exemplary actions of others, such as the poor widow who gave her precious pennies to the temple. At times, his classes involved interactive participation: Heal the sick. Forgive your brother. Seek reconciliation.

I am sure Jesus' disciples were not much different from students today. Each disciple was drawn to one teaching style over another. Peter probably enjoyed a more hands-on approach and enjoyed getting his feet wet. Maybe John preferred to sit with Jesus around the campfire, sharing philosophical ideas or simply enjoying one another's presence. Perhaps Matthew liked rehashing a teaching, pulling out subtle nuances from every telling of the same parable. It would have been disastrous if those disciples refused to receive their Master's teachings just because they weren't presented to them in the manner they preferred. Thank God they chose to stay child-like and teachable!

Years ago, a young artist shared a testimony at the church we both attended. He was eager to share the nugget of wisdom he learned from a First Nations elder. He shared his testimony with the same pride he displayed when discussing one of his art pieces. As he recounted his experience, his eyes glistened from the revelation he received weeks earlier. As the young man wasn't used to speaking in front of a crowd, he rambled on in his nervousness. It would have been easy for some to dismiss his revelation due to his uneasy delivery. Those of us who had ears to hear that day received his truth as our own, and so his seed multiplied. I carry the fruit of his revelation to this day!

Personal Application

Pray with me:

Lord, keep our hearts alert to those moments when You give us the opportunity to learn. Father God, open our eyes so we can see those that You send our way to be our teachers; remove any preconceived ideas that would blind us to the lessons You have for us. Remove from our hearts any prejudice that would place barriers between us and those who carry Your blessings. Keep our hearts, minds, and spirits teachable through Your gentle conviction and encouragement. When we are unreceptive, Holy Spirit, draw our focus back to You.

Not Always All Together

SOMETIMES, AN APOLOGY IS NOT ACCEPTABLE

As a Canadian, I am proud that my nation is known worldwide for our national politeness and tolerance. It is often said that Canadians are so polite that we will apologise to a table if we happen to bump into it. I must confess that I once apologised to my reflection when I accidentally brushed against a mirrored wall. My international friends boast that they can spot a Canadian by our habit of tagging an 'eh' at the end of every sentence and by our need to apologise for everything. Canadians don't say 'eh' as often as other nations insist that we do, however we stand guilty as charged when it comes to apologising way too often.

We are raised to do from an early age. I remember my mother's attempts to distract me from childhood bumps and bruises by suggesting that I consider the feelings of the poor sidewalk I assaulted. Unless I was truly injured, her little plot never failed to get me to giggle at the absurdity of such a request. Her ruse worked just as well with her grandchildren!

In the age of political correctness, Canadians are beside ourselves as we try to keep up with the latest terminology for a people group or a disadvantaged person. Born out of a fear of possibly offending anyone, our national and provincial laws are increasingly restricting our freedom of speech.

One day, I felt the Lord's gentle conviction. I apologise much too much for His liking. I protested. "But I am Canadian!" The Lord didn't let me off the hook. He reminded me of the countless times I offered a hasty apology to avoid confrontation. I would appease a friend rather than speak the truth in love. Apologising in such an instance is akin to lying. It is harmful to the other party, allowing them to maintain the delusion that they are rightfully entitled to their offence.

I run across the easily offended just about everywhere. These folks feel the world owes them an apology, and they have difficulty in discerning what is honestly an offence and what is merely an annoyance. While God calls us to turn the other cheek and to go the extra mile, it is not pleasing to Him when we facilitate boorish behaviour purely out of a fear of rocking the boat. We are called to be humble, gentle, and patient. Above all, we are commanded to be loving. However, we are to speak the truth within the confines of that love.

"When you shoot an arrow of truth, dip its point in honey "- Arab Proverb

Ephesians 4:1-3; 14-16 — "Therefore I, a prisoner for serving the Lord, beg you to lead a life worthy of your calling, for you have been called by God. Always be humble and gentle. Be patient with each other, making allowance for each other's faults because of your love. Make every effort to keep yourselves united in the Spirit, binding yourselves together with peace. …Then we will no longer be immature like children. We won't be tossed and blown about by every wind of new teaching. We will not be influenced when people try to trick us with lies so clever they sound like the truth.

Instead, we will speak the truth in love, growing in every way more and more like Christ, who is the head of his body, the church. He makes the whole body fit together perfectly. As each part does its own special work, it helps the other parts grow, so that the whole body is healthy and growing and full of love."

Personal Application

1. How does being unified in the Spirit and loving one another protect us from being deceived?

2. Read the following quote by Hannah Whithall Smith, then journal, using the questions that follow as prompts.

"If I am walking along the street with a very disfiguring hole in the back of my dress, of which I am in ignorance, it is certainly a very great comfort to me to have a kind friend who will tell me of it. And similarly, it is indeed a comfort to know that there is always abiding with me a divine, all-seeing Comforter, who will reprove me for all my faults, and will not let me go on in a fatal unconsciousness of them."

We all have our blind spots, and we need our brothers and sisters to point out the 'disfiguring holes' in our garments. How well do you receive loving correction? Do you view someone disagreeing with you as rejection? How easily do you take offense?

For further study on the subject, I highly recommend John Bevere's classic, "The Bait of Satan, Living Free from the Deadly Trap of Offense."

WE NEED TO TALK

"It is one of the severest tests of friendship to tell your friend his faults. So, to love a man that you cannot bear to see a stain upon him, and to speak painful truth through loving words, that is friendship." ~ Henry Ward Beecher

Strong, enduring friendships are priceless. I'm not talking about passing acquaintances with whom you share a smile or a handshake at church. Nor am I referring to coworkers with whom you share football scores with during lunch break. I am speaking of those precious gifts God has planted in your life, friends who know you inside out and still love you.

I am talking of those friends in whom you have invested your heart. You've poured out your thoughts, shared your woes, and exposed just about every one of your faults in their presence. You've sat across the table and offered a comforting hand as they shared their pain. These are the type of friends with whom you have howled with laughter at shared memories until your face hurt. I'm talking about the friends who dropped everything to rush to your aid and expected nothing in return.

Such friendships call for ongoing maintenance and open discussion, even when that discussion might be challenging. I had one of those conversations over the phone with a dear friend a few years ago. It called for complete honesty, swathed in God's love and grace. My hand shook as I held the phone to my ear and her voice quivered. We valued our friendship far too much to let it fall apart. We knew we could not cave into fear. Two hours later, we hung up. I was exhausted, and so was she. We came away feeling heard.

A mutual fear we would hurt each other if the truth were spoken crashed down. The strain and distance I had felt between us vanished as we allowed light to expose darkness. I am grateful that a loving God graced us with courage and vulnerability that day. I don't know what I'd do without her.

Personal Application

Is there a friendship in your life that was once strong and healthy? Have you drifted apart and you aren't sure why? Perhaps a misunderstanding built a barrier. Perhaps a silly jealous moment caused distance. Perhaps pride turned your heart cold. Before walking away, consider all you invested in that relationship and how much your friend has invested in you.

Be the first to take that step toward transparent reconciliation. Invite that friend into an open dialogue. Make sure that invitation is expressed in humility, spoken in love, and infused with courage to speak what needs to be said. Don't let a heart-cherished relationship wither away.

Be careful to remove any rubble that blocks communication.

Isaiah 62:10 – "Go through, go through the gates; prepare the way for the people; build up, build up the highway; clear it of stones; lift up a signal over the peoples."

LORD, CONSTRAIN WHAT NEEDS TO BE CONSTRAINED

"We have a choice. We can carry the world on our shoulders, or we can say, 'I give up Lord; here's my life. I give you my world, the whole world.'" ~ Bruce Larson, "Believe and Belong" Power Books

My deadliest foe is the fear of man. While my heart cries out for a fresh wind of the Spirit to sweep over my friends and family, I whisper a postscript. "But please, please Jesus, don't make the process too messy and unpredictable!"

My church is known for our exuberant worship. We actively pursue intimacy with God, and we embrace those with the same heart to join us in that pursuit. We welcome those who are not yet believers, those who might hold misperceptions about Christianity, and those who are merely curious. Therein lays the crux of my problem.

I ask the Lord to bring comfort, healing, and restoration as a young man weeps uncontrollably under God's loving touch at the altar. At the same time, I sense that his weeping is giving some newcomers a bit of concern. I am tempted to ask the Lord to tone it down so as not to offend those who don't yet understand what is taking place. I cheer on the joy-filled dance of a young woman who experienced a significant victory after a long battle. Yet, I hope the dance doesn't provide more evidence to the sceptic sitting in the back row, reinforcing his misbelief that Christianity is only for the emotionally unsound.

Faced with such a dilemma one Sunday morning, I confessed to the Lord that I didn't know how to pray. In response, God reminded me that He is the Lord of all. His reputation did not need defending. As I quieted my heart, I prayed a silent prayer, "Lord, constrain what should be constrained and release what should be released."

As I prayed, my anxiety lessened. God was, and is, and always will be in control. Although my prayer was at first targeted toward those around me, I became aware that my prayer was more for me than anyone else.

"Lord, constrain what must be constrained in me. I lay my fears and my anxieties at your feet. I place my trust in this truth - You are good. You know each heart, and you know just what each heart needs. I rest in your peace."

Personal Application

What worries do you need to lay at the foot of the cross today? Spend a few moments right now and lay them down. Ask Holy Spirit to convict you if you try to pick those worries up again.

LEAVE DEMOLITION TO THE EXPERT

When someone has a mindset so ingrained that it is a part of their mental fibre, only a miracle can break through the walls of delusion that they built.

It is painful to watch when someone close to us suffers the consequences of a deliberately chosen mindset. We love these people! It hurts to watch them struggle. However, experience teaches us that we make things worse by attempting to break down the walls of deception with earthly wisdom, logic, and counsel. We can't allow our fleshly brilliant 'fix-the-world' tendencies to kick into gear; we must bite our tongues.

So, what can we do? I include myself in this question!

We must cooperate with Holy Spirit and allow Him to lead. We need to give Him the room necessary to lead those we love into freedom. As we do, He provides us with two powerful tools: prayer and unconditional love. As we pray, Holy Spirit patiently begins His work, using gracious love and conviction. He eases past self-defense mechanisms, breaking through hardened mortar of fear and bricks of self-deception. As we love, we provide a place where they can ask their questions free from any fear of rejection or condemnation.

2 Corinthians 10: 3-5 — *"For though we walk in the flesh, we are not waging war according to the flesh. For the weapons of our warfare are not of the flesh but have divine power to destroy strongholds. We destroy arguments and every lofty opinion raised against the knowledge of God, and take every thought captive to obey Christ."*

2 Timothy 2:23-26 — *"Have nothing to do with foolish, ignorant controversies; you know that they breed quarrels. And the Lord's servant must not be quarrelsome but kind to everyone, able to teach, patiently enduring evil, correcting his opponents with gentleness. God may perhaps grant them repentance leading to a knowledge of the truth, and they may come to their senses and escape from the snare of the devil, after being captured by him to do his will."*

Personal Application

As you read the bible passages above, what key points stand out to you?

1. How can you practically implement these truths?
2. What can you start doing today?
3. What do you need to stop doing today?

If you are a 'fixer' by nature, memorise these Bible passages.

PICKING UP OFFENSES?

Proverbs 19:11 — "Good sense makes one slow to anger, and it is his glory to overlook an offense."

I first met Tom at a church we both attended. Tom has a slight physical disability. He also lives with learning disabilities, and a couple of mental disorders that are easily managed by medication. Tom has the aura of child-like innocence and trust. His large brown eyes peer innocently at the world through thick-lensed glasses.

You might assume that this precious child of God has led a sheltered life. This assumption would be wrong. In his early teens, Tom's parents kicked him out of their home, citing their inability to cope with his behaviour problems. As a result, he ended up on the street. The Lord protected him from drug addiction, but Tom was abused and mistreated by many of those who he innocently befriended. Yet somehow, his heart remained soft, and Tom became a Christian through an outreach programme to homeless youth.

God's family became Tom's family. Various ministries in the downtown core watched out for him. For several years, Tom lived in a number of government-sponsored housing projects, until he was blessed to move to a safer neighbourhood, sharing a house with several Christian men. His nightmare years on the street were behind him, and he only ventured downtown to volunteer in faith-based soup kitchens.

Right before Tom moved into his new home, he began attending a fellowship I led in my apartment. Every week, he arrived a good half hour before our group started. I was usually busy with last minute preparations, and so I would leave him to his own devices after making sure he was comfortable. I often found him gazing out my balcony window. I assumed he was enjoying the picturesque view. One week, I casually mentioned how beautiful the river valley looked far below. Tom looked back at me, startled from his thoughts.

He pointed to the apartment building across the street, matter-of-factly informing me that his parents lived in that building. Wistfully, Tom admitted that he hadn't seen his mother in seven or eight years. Before I could respond, he hastily informed me that he saw his father every year on his birthday. Every couple of years, he would meet his dad on Christmas Eve for lunch at a diner in the downtown core. His father would even pay for his meal.

My heart broke as I felt anger well up inside me. How could parents abandon their disabled son? How could they erase him from their lives? I was ready to march over to that building and give them a piece of my mind, but Tom's expression stopped me. There wasn't a hint of anger, bitterness, or resentment in his face or his tone. His mental disabilities were mild enough that he understood his parents abandoned him.

However, Tom's heart was free of the dark emotions that rushed over me.

He had made his peace long ago and had forgiven his parents. There was nothing but unconditional love in Tom's heart for them. He admitted to me that he was difficult as a teen.

I watched this young man walk out Christ's example, "Forgive them, Father, they do not know what they do." (Luke 23:24) Humbled, I let go of my resentment. If Tom no longer battled, why should I? I learned an invaluable lesson that night. The battle belongs to the Lord. Tom had stepped aside in his battle, and so should I.

I am clannish at heart, and most of my friends would say one of my prominent character traits is loyalty. Although loyalty is a noble quality to foster, resentment and bitterness toward those who hurt my family and friends are not so noble.

I yielded the ugly side of my clannish nature to God. In return, He gave me opportunities to extend unconditional love and grace to those who have hurt my friends. I learned to stop being a guard dog over the hearts of my friends, and I learned to allow the Lord to be their protector and the lifter of their heads.

———————

Personal Application

Is there is someone in your life who has forgiven their offender and moved on, but you have yet to forgive their offender as well? Take a moment to confess that unforgiveness to the Lord. Allow His peace to fill your heart so you can be a powerful support to your friend.

SOMETIMES, A MESS MUST BE MADE

Proverbs 14:4 – "Without oxen a stable stays clean, but you need a strong ox for a large harvest."

At one point in my life, it wasn't uncommon for my kitchen to go unused for days at a time. As a result, my stove top burner rings were spotless. My counter tops rarely needed more than a quick wipe with a dishcloth. I swept my floor perhaps once a week. My kitchen's pristine condition, however, changed for the worse one Saturday afternoon.

It was a friend's birthday, and I promised to bring a side dish to a potluck we were having in her honour. I was confident that I could find something suitable at my local deli counter, but after fruitlessly roaming up and down the display case, my confidence plummeted. I revved my power chair into high gear and sped around the aisles in a panic as I now had less than ninety minutes before the party. After gathering a few random ingredients, I raced home. By the time I arrived there, I would have 45 minutes to put something together.

As soon as I stepped in the door, bowls flew, graters grated, cans opened, bags ripped open, and vegetables were tossed. My pepper mill was empty. As I refilled it, peppercorns bounced across the floor. A can's lid landed soupy side down on the counter, causing cream of mushroom soup to drip over the edge. Realising I had no time to put the casserole in the oven, I chose to use my microwave instead. As I reached to turn off the oven, I knocked over a loosely capped salt shaker.

As soon as the dish was hot, I wrapped it in a towel and reached for my coat and cane. I sighed as I turned out the lights and headed out the door. I knew there would be a huge mess to deal with later. I was already tired. As an introvert, I knew I would be exhausted by the time I arrived home. I love my friends, but parties tire me out!

The dinner was a success. Laughter, gentle ribbing, tales of our shared past, and good food were passed back and forth across the table. My friend was blessed as one of her greatest pleasures was to have a leisurely meal at home. Her friends were just as blessed. It had been a long while since we had last gathered.

Five hours later, I returned to my messy kitchen. Cheese encrusted the grater. Dried soup splattered the backsplash of my kitchen counter. I stepped on something sticky and gingerly removed my shoes so as not to spread the goo. I re-entered the disaster area in my stocking feet, only to step on a stray peppercorn. Ouch!

As I hobbled down the hall in search of a broom, I realised something had shifted in my heart. My kitchen certainly hadn't been visited by an army of cleaning elves while I was out. My circumstances hadn't changed, but my attitude had. I no longer saw the looming task as a wearisome chore. Although I was exhausted, the clean-up was a joy as I remembered how quickly my friends devoured my simple dish at the dinner party. Little did they know the damage I caused to my apartment in the making of that casserole!

Working for the Lord is often a messy venture. It's not easy dealing with people who have messy lives while I try to clean up my own messes. And yet, sometimes a mess needs to be made if there is to be a blessing.

For those who might be curious, here is the recipe for my dish. I left out the instructions for dropping lids and peppercorns and splattering back splashes. Feel free to add your own creative flair to the recipe.

Katherine's Green Bean Casserole

Ingredients:

- 4 cups frozen French-cut green beans
- 1 cup frozen bell pepper strips
- One small onion sliced and cut into strips
- 1 ½ cup grated cheddar cheese
- One can cream of mushroom and garlic soup
- Sea salt and freshly ground black pepper to taste
- 3 tbsp. toasted, slivered almonds

Method:

- Use fresh vegetables if possible.

- If you use frozen vegetables, rinse and drain well, then pat dry.

- Mix the first six ingredients together, reserving a ½ cup cheese.

- Sprinkle the remaining cheese on top, then bake in a 350 oven for 20 minutes or until the cheese is golden brown and the casserole is bubbly hot.

- Sprinkle almonds over the dish before serving.

Personal Application

Find meaning in your messes. If your house is chaotic and disorganised as you hear the raucous laughter of healthy children at play, you are doing a good job, Moms and Dads.

Keep your eyes focused on the end goal. Sometimes, a mess needs to be made to reach it.

Be as accepting of the messes in your own life as you are of the messes in other people's lives.

Don't allow perfectionism to stop you from ministering to others through hospitality.

Practical Tip: Always have a Plan B in mind for potlucks!

THANKS, SPIRITUAL MOMS AND DADS

Thank you, spiritual moms and dads, who nurtured, comforted, and encouraged me in my walk. They held me accountable while demonstrating unconditional love. Without their influence, I would have been lost as a new believer! I had no idea how to feed myself; I had no idea how to dive into the Bible and receive nourishment there.

I didn't know what it meant to have a pure heart and clean hands before the Lord. The idea of daily repentance was foreign to me. These cherished brothers and sisters pointed me to the Comforter and my Protector, my Best Friend and my Redeemer, Jesus Christ. They demonstrated His love, security, and acceptance through warm hugs, listening ears, and wise counsel.

Opal was a particularly much-loved spiritual mom of mine. This amazing woman invited me into her heart as a daughter for a couple of years in my late teens. I trekked to her home at least two or three times a week, not minding the long bus ride across town. I loved to sit in Opal's kitchen; she was always cooking or baking. I felt free to chat about my day, and she would pick up cues in my conversation, asking leading questions without me realising I was being led!

Time would get away from us, and Opal would insist I stay for supper. I related to her family; they weren't perfect; they were just everyday folk like me. She had a backslidden son, a non-believing husband, and a daughter whose faith often wavered. To call their tiny house modest was an understatement, yet Opal made room for me.

Over the period of several months, Opal led me into a deeper walk with Christ. I learned more in her kitchen than I would have by reading countless books on discipleship. By infusing the principles of forgiveness, accountability, and faith into our conversations, she taught me to clothe myself in the garments of praise and righteousness. I learned about prayer, intercession, and personal healing ministry.

Recognising my budding spiritual gifts, she and her ministry partner mentored me. They invited me to observe as they ministered to hurting young men and women who attended our weekly interdenominational home fellowship. Many of these young people were living in a Christian Halfway House ministry they oversaw. Opal and her partner guided me as I began to pray for others, always giving encouraging feedback. When needed, they provided gentle correction without any judgment or shaming involved, and it was always done in a loving and honouring manner.

Opal was just one of many spiritual moms in my life, and I've had many spiritual dads as well. How grateful I am to them! I now have the awesome privilege to act as a mentor and spiritual mom to many. I hope to pass on even a small measure of the positive impact my mentors have had on my life.

Personal Application

Perhaps as you read this, the name of a new believer in your church or faith community flashes in your mind. Is God calling you to mentor this person, nurture their faith, and draw them into a deeper walk with our Heavenly Father?

Are you looking for a spiritual parent? Be a good son or daughter first. Be receptive to input from unlikely sources; be open and friendly to the faithful in your body. Volunteer for tasks that no one else will do at church and in your community; that's where you'll find the hidden gold! Those people who sacrifice their time through selfless service make the best role models. The mentors who carried the most weight in my life have not written books; they aren't pastors of mega-churches, and they aren't wealthy business owners. They are everyday saints who loved well during difficult circumstances.

Not Always All Together

A LIFE WELL LIVED

Several years ago, I was honoured to support two sisters as they took care of their father in his final days. Ben passed away surrounded by his children and loving wife of 53 years. Although the family grieved their loss, they rejoiced that he was finally free of pain. All who knew him had no doubt that Ben was now with his dearest Friend and Saviour.

It might sound strange, but I found Ben's funeral to be inspiring. It was clear that Ben was a man who lived his life well. With humour and passion, Ben raised his five children to love God first and to love other people well. He taught them to be independent, but to temper that independence with compassion. Ben mentored his grandchildren, lavishing love, prayer, and affection on each one. Ben continued to be a loving influence over his family, even as he battled cancer. He shared the following sage advice at a large family gathering that took place a few months before his death. "Live every day in celebration of the life God has given us."

The officiant of the funeral admitted Ben taught him far more than he ever taught Ben. He treasured the wise counsel that this man of God offered him and talked about the rare gift that Ben was to him. Family members gave thanks for their father and grandfather who demonstrated the unconditional love of God. The sincerity of their words was shown in their laughter and tears.

After the celebration of Ben's life, a luncheon was served. An open microphone was placed at the front of the hall, and the stories began to flow. As someone once said, the church was sold out, and the only seat I could find was on the platform, behind the podium. From my little cubbyhole, I listened as person after person spoke.

A young man choked back tears as he talked about the unreserved love that he received from Ben. Even during full blown teenage angst and rebellion, he looked forward to coming to church. He knew Ben would be there to greet him. A couple struggled through their tears and their limited English to speak of the friendship Ben and his wife extended them when they first arrived in our country. Ben's former employees spoke of his outstanding leadership and the example he set by his work ethic. They were thankful for Ben's insistence that they produce a product in which they could take pride. Four hours after the service began, people still wanted to speak. As the church needed for another purpose, we reluctantly dispersed.

I never met Ben; I only attended his funeral as a prayer support for his daughters. By the end of that day, I felt I had known this man for years through the joyous God-centred testimonies that were shared.

Hebrews 12:1-2 — "Therefore, since we are surrounded by so great a cloud of witnesses, let us also lay aside every weight, and sin which clings so closely, and let us run with endurance the race that is set before us, looking to Jesus, the founder and perfecter of our faith, who for the joy that was set before him endured the cross, despising the shame, and is seated at the right hand of the throne of God."

You ran a good race, Ben. I pray that when my earthly life is over, people will be able to say the same about me.

Personal Application

Legacy. A word usually used to describe the foundation someone of Ben's age passes down to the generations that follow them. However, I don't think we don't have to wait until the end of our days to pass on a legacy.

My church rents facilities in a school. We keep a simple mantra in mind as we tear down our equipment and put away the chairs every Sunday. "Leave the gym in better shape than how it was when we arrived."

If life circumstances took you away from your city, church or job, what legacy would you like to leave behind? What are some practical ideas you can start applying today that will leave your sphere of influence in better shape than it was when your arrived?

A WALK TO THE BEACH

"Let's have a picnic in the Redwood Forest, and we'll see the Oregon Coast on the way!" Although it was hours out of our way, my travel companions and I just could not allow that tempting invitation to pass us by. We found ourselves following our friend's SUV along a winding highway from north-central California down to the Pacific Coast.

The desert-like terrain of Shasta County slowly gave way to lush undergrowth and small evergreens, and soon, we were driving along the famous Pacific Coast Highway. We pulled into the nearest state park. Two teens who were travelling with us sprinted up a well-worn path, calling back over their shoulders. "Come on; the ocean is out there!"

By the time I pulled myself out of the car, they were out of sight. As I approached the path, I saw a mountain of powder-soft sand. I knew there was no way I could navigate the route without help. My cane proved useless, and the thought of dragging my walker over the dunes was laughable.

I gratefully accepted the steady arm of a friend, but after a few stumbling steps, I knew I would not make the distance, even with her help. Disappointment washed over me. I so wanted to see the ocean. I also knew if I returned to the car, my kind-hearted friends would cut short their time on the beach. They would feel terrible knowing that I was sitting by myself in a drab parking lot.

Another friend saw my dilemma and came along to help. Using my friends as a steadying support, I slowly made my way across the dunes, step by difficult step. I kept my focus on our travelling companions in the distance as they frolicked on the beach. I trudged on.

The moment we reached the well-packed sand, I urged my helpers to join the others who were dancing along the shoreline. I stayed far back from the water as I needed to protect my braces, but I was close enough to call back and forth to my friends. The scent of the sea breeze was intoxicating, and a low mist rolled in off the ocean, creating a magical moment. Cue three horses and their riders appearing out of the fog, galloping across the sand between me and my companions. It felt like a scene in a Hollywood movie.

The walk back to the parking lot was just as gruelling, and I was extremely fatigued. Halfway back to the car, we switched helpers who were closer to my height, making the trek a little easier. By the time we reached the parking lot, I was exhausted to the point of trembling. But I was full of gratitude. I saw the ocean!

If I hadn't reached out for help from my friends and if they had not been attentive to my needs, we all would have missed an incredible experience. I would have been stuck in the parking lot, and they would have shortened their stay on the beach.

A few days later, one of my travel companions shared her testimony at our church. She gave thanks for the healing that she received as a member of a loving and supportive body of believers. She acknowledged all those who walked beside her during challenging times. It was bittersweet as my friend would soon be moving thousands of miles away. We gathered as a congregation to pray for her. My pastor ended our time of prayer asking us a rhetorical question. "How could anyone ever say they don't need the church?"

Indeed, how could anyone say they can do this Christian walk on their own? I know I can't.

Personal Application

I planned our road trip months in advance, complete with road maps, driving distances, hotel rooms, and dinner arrangements! Once we arrived at our destination, I took off my navigator's cap and enjoyed my freedom. My friends teased me with mock dismay. They now had to take the reins! I think they were surprised that I was so willing to abandon my travel plans for our first travel day back home. Little did they know that travelling the Pacific Highway was on my bucket list.

If you tend to micromanage your life, how flexible are you willing to be? Do you miss the promptings of Holy Spirit because you think you are a better planner than He is? Try to be spontaneous, even if you must plan for it. That's a joke!

Our fun on the beach would have been short lived if I hadn't made my need known and if my friends hadn't met that need. We need one another. Does pride get in your way? Are you isolated because you haven't reached out for help? Is there someone you haven't seen at church for a while and who you know doesn't have transportation? Call them up and see if they need a ride!

Confessions of a Relentless Cheerleader

1 Thessalonians 5:11 — "Therefore encourage one another and build one another up, just as you are doing."

Although I am not much of a sports fan, my inner cheerleader emerges at every opportunity. I am an encourager at heart. Nothing gives me more pleasure than to celebrate the determination and hard work that leads to victories in my friends' lives. I will pull out my spiritual pom-poms to celebrate any victory, no matter how small it might be.

Speaking a right word of prophetic encouragement helps others to mine for gold. Sometimes, we shovel past a lot of dirt before we find the first shiny nuggets. Eventually, we'll hit the mother-lode!

Kris Vallotton, a respected prophetic voice, puts it this way, "*The gift of prophecy is not simply patting people on the back, telling them nice things about themselves, and pretending that there is nothing negative in their lives. Instead, prophetic words are so supernaturally powerful that they can actually unearth the gold in the hearts of people—gold that is hidden under the dirt of their lives.* This often displaces their confusion and delivers them from guilt, shame, and sin." - Vallotton, Kris. *Basic Training for the Prophetic Ministry, Expanded Edition.* Shippensburg, PA: Destiny Image Pub, 2015. Print.

Gold miners don't focus on the dirt they displace to find gold. I like that analogy. While the dirt in the lives of others might capture the attention of some, my eye is drawn to the valuable nuggets in my friends' lives. I take advantage of every opportunity to call attention to the gold, even if those friends don't want to admit it is there.

I love to speak truth-infused, life-giving encouragement. On the other hand, I am careful not to mislead others by speaking kind words that have no basis in truth. I wouldn't tell a tone-deaf friend they have a voice of an angel, but I have passed on a message from God to tone-deaf friends that they make their heavenly Father's heart swell with delight as they display uninhibited worship.

Unfortunately, many in the body of Christ take Paul's exhortation to "Speak the truth in love" as a free license to bring a word of correction. However, when that passage is read in context, you realise Paul was not speaking of correction at all! He was speaking of the mutual building up of the Body through exhortation, teaching and most of all, love. The Body of Christ falls short in 'speaking the truth in love' with words of encouragement that celebrate the victories and exposes the gold in each of us. Correction is necessary at times, but I firmly believe regular encouragement is vital for the health of every believer.

Paul refers to the Christian journey as a race. Earthly marathoners rely on the cheers of the crowds when they hit the infamous wall of pain, miles before the finish line. They don't need a critique of what they are doing wrong. They need words that speak life. They need to be reminded they trained to overcome that very moment. They can do this!

Ephesians 4:15-16 — "Speaking the truth in love, we are to grow up in every way into him who is the head, into Christ, from whom the whole body, joined and held together by every joint with which it is equipped, when each part is working properly, makes the body grow so that it builds itself up in love."

Personal Application

It will take practice to see the gold in others if you have been accustomed to examining dirt piles. Look for opportunities to point out admirable character traits. If your friend is discouraged, remind them of obstacles they have overcome. Don't flatter!

When critiquing someone's performance, always highlight the good first. Be specific! If you lead a prayer team, for example, and a member of that team isn't following protocol, the conversation might look like this: "I loved the way you honoured that woman as you prayed for her. I could see you were full of faith!" Let the praise sink in before continuing. "You did a great job! However, there was one thing I was wondering about. I noticed you placed your hand on her shoulder as you were interviewing her. Did I miss when you asked her permission to do so first?"

Not Always All Together

RECEIVE GIFTS GRACIOUSLY

In the early years of my parent's marriage, my father's question, 'What do you want as a gift?' was always met with a pensive sigh from my mother, 'Surprise me.' After several such surprises, my mother begrudgingly gave her hapless husband a list of items that she would like. After many disappointments, she further refined the list by prioritising the items from the most-wanted to the least-wanted. Year after year, my father would somehow get it wrong, and my mother chose not to hide her disapproval.

When I was in the fourth grade, my dad decided I was old enough to tag along on his annual Christmas-shopping trip. Perhaps he thought a ten-year-old female would understand the mystique of a grown woman better than he did. As we pulled up to our local discount department store, I knew my father had made his first mistake. When we headed toward the household section, I whistled under my breath. "Mistake number two, Dad!" Looking up into my father's earnest face and then looking down at his white-knuckled hands clenched onto the shopping cart in front of him, I wisely kept my peace.

I shook my head in disbelief as he loaded the cart with three-dozen cheap coffee mugs. Coffee mugs were indeed on the list my mother provided, the third or fourth item below books and bubble bath. I suppose he guessed that if he purchased enough mugs during one expedition, he'd never have to go through the torment of buying mugs again in his lifetime.

The year he came home with a dozen large ashtrays whose uneven bottoms scratched my mother's coffee table should perhaps wisely stay in the dark annals of unfortunate gift purchases. Upon the arrival of gift certificates, my father's gift-buying trips slowly faded away.

My dad was a generous man, and he was the first to reach into his pocket to give to a friend or family member in need, even if it meant giving the last dollar in his wallet. I accompanied him on various gift-buying missions; he never conveyed any resentment toward my mother. I always felt his anxiety. He wanted to please my mom with the perfect gift at least once in his life! His intention was to bless her – even if it killed him.

I was once guilty of placing pressure on friends and family, expecting them to love me in what I felt was a perfect way. I subconsciously expected them to say just the right words and bestow on me the most thoughtful of sentiments. I became increasingly disappointed, resentful, and hurt over what I perceived to be thoughtlessness on their part. Although I was careful not to show my disappointment, I know I hurt the feelings of the more sensitive among my family and friends.

After one particularly painful birthday party, the Lord exposed my ungrateful heart, and I repented. Behind that ungrateful heart was a wound that went back to early childhood, and I allowed the Lord's healing hand to touch that memory. At last, my heart was opened to receive the love that was behind every gift given. I was free to see the generous spirits of my friends and family. Since then, I can happily say that as I continue to grow in this area of my life, disappointments fade away. I have a deeper awareness of the daily blessings that the Lord brings my way.

"We prevent God from giving us the great spiritual gifts He has in store for us, because we do not give thanks for daily gifts. We think we dare not be satisfied with the small measure of spiritual knowledge, experience, and love that has been given to us, and that we must constantly be looking forward eagerly for the highest good. Then we deplore the fact that we lack the deep certainty, the strong faith, and the rich experience that God has given to others, and we consider this lament to be pious. We pray for the big things and forget to give thanks for the ordinary, small (and yet really not small) gifts. How can God entrust great things to one who will not thankfully receive from Him the little things?" Dietrich Bonhoeffer, *"Life Together: The Classic Exploration of Faith in Community"* Harper Collins Publishers

---

Personal Application

Here are a few questions to ask yourself.

1. How well do you receive gifts?
2. Are you constantly let-down on holidays and special occasions?

3. Do you expect others to guess at what you want? Do you then blame them when they get it wrong?

4. Do you feel it cheapens a gift if you must tell someone what you want?

5. Do you secretly feel jealous when others receive blessings that you have not yet received?

6. Do you see yourself as an orphan in God's orphanage or do you see yourself as the cherished adopted child of a generous Father who always has more than enough?

TREASURE YOUR INHERITANCE

I loved my grandmother, and she loved me. When I was a child, my family enjoyed visiting her in the Okanogan Valley of British Columbia, a region recognised for its recreational lakes and its incredible bounty of seasonal fruits. Through a remarkable set of circumstances, my grandmother drew close to God in her mid-seventies. It was my great joy to watch her grow in her faith, and we kept in touch through letters and the occasional phone call as I travelled with Youth With A Mission.

One summer, in between missionary assignments, I was delighted when my grandmother invited me to spend a week with her. By then, she was well into retirement, and we enjoyed many leisurely chats over tea that was served in her bone china tea service. Although I admired the china, I begged for a kitchen mug. I was too nervous to drink from one of the delicate tea cups. My grandmother, knowing my propensity for dropping things, agreed that my suggestion was a sound one, and so we compromised. I drank from a sturdier mug that was classy enough to fit the elegant theme of our grown-up tea parties.

I knew my grandmother treasured that tea set. A close friend gave it to her in gratitude for the nursing care my grandmother provided her. When my grandmother moved back to Alberta to be closer to her family, she settled into a studio apartment in a seniors retirement centre. Although she parted ways with most of her possessions, the tea service stayed with her. While it sat untouched on her shelf, it still brightened her room, and I admired it every time I visited.

Shortly after my grandmother's death, I was both touched and terrified to learn that she passed on the tea service to me. I kept the set on display for a couple of years. Over time, I began to notice a few fine cracks on some of the cups, caused by my less-than-graceful dusting techniques. I packed it away with the help of a friend, then placed the box beyond my clumsy reach. Several years later, I passed the set down to my niece, who never had the chance to meet her great-grandmother. I made sure that when a family member delivered the tea service to her that he passed along its story as well. It is my hope that my niece will treasure the set as much as I do and maybe one day pass it down to the next generation.

Hopefully, my niece will take better care of her inheritance than the children of Israel took care of theirs. Much like my niece, the children of Israel were blessed with a precious legacy. As I read the latter chapters of the book of Joshua and the entire book of Judges, I am struck by the apparent disconnect between the generations that immediately followed the first settlers of the Promised Land. How quickly they forgot their story! The horrifying consequences of that disconnect carried down generations after them. God admonished the Israelites through Moses to pass on the traditions and rules for living to the following generations. Perhaps, Joshua and his cohorts neglected to pass on that sense of urgency to the next generation.

Deuteronomy 11:18-21 — "You shall therefore lay up these words of mine in your heart and in your soul, and you shall bind them as a sign on your hand, and they shall be as frontlets between your eyes. You shall teach them to your children, talking of them when you are sitting in your house, and when you are walking by the way, and when you lie down, and when you rise. You shall write them on the doorposts of your house and on your gates, that your days and the days of your children may be multiplied in the land that the Lord swore to your fathers to give them, as long as the heavens are above the earth."

Did Caleb and Joshua model a deep sense of gratitude to God to their children and grandchildren? How then did the next generation develop a culture of entitlement so quickly? Soon after Joshua's generation passed away, the subsequent generation lost interest in protecting the culture of their ancestors. They allowed other religious practices to bump against their own, and each point of contact caused minute fractures that eventually stole their inheritance and sullied their faith. Within three or four generations, the children of Israel found themselves in slavery once again, the forewarned aftermath of their failure to follow the law.

Personal Application

As you think about the first generations of Israelites in the Promised Land, ask yourself the following questions:

1. Am I a good steward of the spiritual inheritance passed down to

me?

2. Is my understanding of the ways of God solely based on sermons, books, and conferences?

3. Do I maintain a current relationship with God through personal worship, prayer, and Bible study?

4. Do I set an example for the next generation that will give them a model to build upon so they can expand the spiritual inheritance I will pass down to them?

5. Do I exhibit gratefulness?

6. Do I share my testimonies of God's faithfulness?

MEET SOMEONE ELSE

John 13:14 – "If I then, your Lord and Teacher, have washed your feet, you also ought to wash one another's feet."

It had been a long day. The disciples were looking forward to a quiet dinner with their Master. They walked with Him in the crowded streets and meeting places of Jerusalem since morning. The day had been an odd one; Jesus spoke of many matters that gave them cause to wonder. Yes, a pleasant meal with friends would be a blessing. They needed time to reorganise and reenergise. They needed time to reflect upon and digest all the exciting events of the day.

Peter and John had gone ahead to prepare for the Passover meal. There was a light at the top of the stairs welcoming the Master and the other disciples as they entered the upper room. The men removed their sandals just outside the door and swept off the dust of the day from the hems of their robes. The aroma of roast lamb combined with the fragrances of the traditional herbs and spices greeted them, invoking memories of Passovers past. More than a few of the disciples felt a little homesick. Each made their way to the dinner table carrying their private worries, joys, and expectations.

In their preoccupation with grumbling stomachs, dark thoughts, and homesickness, the disciples failed to assign a mundane job. Perhaps Peter and John didn't hire enough servants; maybe their Master asked them not to hire anyone extra that evening. Nevertheless, the task remained undone until Jesus hiked up His robes, rolled up His sleeves and wrapped an apron around His waist. It was not until He knelt by Peter with a bowl of water and a towel that His disciples realised just what He was doing. Foot washing was a chore left to a servant or a child. Foot-washing duties were certainly not intended to be left to the Master. Here He was, kneeling in front of Peter, about to do a thankless chore they all assumed would be taken care of by someone else.

When Jesus invited His disciples to follow His example, He was not asking them to add a new ritual to the Passover. He was asking them to step past their perceived needs and serve one another. Jesus knew what lay before Him. He knew that within 24 hours, He would pay the penalty for the sins of His disciples. Jesus knew His friends were more than capable of washing feet. Their problems were wispy clouds in a blue sky compared to the thunderclouds that loomed over Him. And yet, Jesus quietly did the task no one else thought to do; washing hot, dusty, stinky feet.

While His self-absorbed disciples assumed Someone Else would do it, Jesus embodied Someone Else.

Personal Application

Be a Someone Else today. Accept Jesus' invitation, "Come, follow me." Hike up your robe, tie an apron around your waist, and take the posture of a servant.

There will be plenty of opportunities to serve if you have eyes to see and ears to hear.

WE ALWAYS HAVE A CHOICE

"God of our life, there are days when the burdens we carry chafe our shoulders and weigh us down; when the road seems dreary and endless, the skies gray and threatening; when our lives have no music in them, and our hearts are lonely, and our souls have lost their courage. Flood the path with light, run our eyes to where the skies are full of promise; tune our hearts to brave music; give us the sense of comradeship with heroes and saints of every age; and so quicken our spirits that we may be able to encourage the souls of all who journey with us on the road of life, to Your honour and glory." ~ Augustine

In August of 2005, my heart grieved over the devastating aftermath of Hurricane Katrina. I clung to the Lord like a bewildered child. I couldn't wrap my mind around the horrific chaos that followed the storm. He carried me safe in His arms as I prayed, but He didn't shield me. Nor did He shield the rest of the world. We saw it all - good and bad.

Much of the initial response to Hurricane Katrina's devastation was horrifically ugly. News reports exposed insensitivity, slowness of federal aid, hatred, anger, violence, bigotry, corruption, looting of stores for luxury items, desertion of duty, and murder. There were shouts of accusation and there were angry, defensive responses in return. Humanity displayed at its worst.

Philippians 2:4 — "Let each of you look not only to his own interests but also to the interests of others."

I also saw Christ's light shining brightly. Men sacrificed their lives so others might live. Christians led prayer services, they then went beyond prayer by protecting and comforting their fellow New Orleanians in the filth of the Super Dome. Trapped in the middle of chaos, Christians took their place of spiritual authority. They invited others into makeshift sanctuaries under bridges and on street corners. Men stood guard so mothers and children could sleep. What little food that was safe to eat was gathered and then distributed to whomever was in a safe walking distance.

When calamities sweep over us and our communities, we have no choice but to walk through the aftermath of that disaster. Circumstances might lead us to poverty, disability, financial ruin, or the trauma of losing loved ones. As Christ-followers, we cannot allow tragedy to cause our hearts to become bitter. The choices we make following a calamity will either close or open our spirits to God's direction and heart for our communities.

Personal Application

It has been said, "Calamity does not build character, it reveals character." The building blocks of character are made from the choices we make each day.

Learn to respond with patience, tolerance, and compassion to the petty annoyances that come your way each day.

Keep your eyes open for small opportunities to serve strangers.

Be a person of your word. Be swift to follow through on any offer you make to help.

Invest yourself in the appearance of your community. Take part in organized clean-up campaigns.

Get to know the people on your block well enough that you are aware of their daily comings and goings. Shovel snow from your neighbour's sidewalks or offer to mow their lawn once or twice a year.

Welcome newcomers to your neighbourhood.

Let people into traffic, keep your hands on the steering wheel and off the horn.

Practice self-discipline in situations that tend to press all your buttons. Watch your inner dialogue, don't judge or complain in your thought life.

Be patient while waiting at the checkout, especially if the person holding up the line has a disability or is elderly.

If you notice that someone has been missing from church for a while, call them, but don't call from a motivation to drag them back to church. Ask if they need any practical help or prayer.

It is the Thought That Counts

"A Christian should always remember that the value of his good works is not based on their number and excellence, but on the love of God which prompts him to do these things." - John of the Cross

Have you ever been the victim of a drive-by attack of kindness that left you with a bad taste in your mouth and confusion in your spirit? I have been both the victim and the perpetrator of such an assault.

If we attach conditions to our actions, then our actions are done with questionable motivations. In the past, I was guilty of doing something kind to make a point. This passive-aggressive behaviour is devious. While my victims might have sensed something stunk but they weren't sure where the source of the stench.

Several years ago, I hosted a potluck. At the end of the meal, the kitchen was a mess and dessert needed to be served. The conversation around the table was light-hearted and casual. After what I felt was a reasonable time for people to sit around the table chatting, I started clearing dishes, assuming no one else was going to step up to the plate. On the surface, my table clearing was a gracious act. I was serving my fellow brothers and sisters in Christ.

However, if you looked carefully, you would have seen the look of martyrdom on my face. Even those with the dullest of hearing could hear my weary sigh as I noisily gathered mugs from the table and dumped them in the sink. Not a word did I speak, but my actions screamed my moral superiority over the lazy oafs who dared linger around the table after a meal. In my friends' defence, my attitude probably stifled any inclination they had to help me in the kitchen.

Perhaps you've heard the tale of the ever-loving wife who delicately released a moan as she bent over to pick up her husband's socks. "No, no, dear. I insist. You go right ahead and watch your little football game. After all, I only have to put Sunday dinner on the table and take care of the baby." After a significant pause, she offered, ever so sweetly. "Would you like your favourite layer cake for dessert?" Oh, be wary of that blade that slices through the promised cake! It might just as well be in her husband's back, given her deep resentment.

Passive-aggressive behaviour cuts deep into a victim's heart, causing festering wounds. Such conduct is contaminated with poisonous resentment, bitterness, and maliciousness.

When we are displeased or disappointed, we must speak the truth in love. By stating our needs and concerns without manipulation, we give others permission to meet those needs if they so choose.

I'm sure I missed out on a good conversation over that sink of hot, soapy suds when all I needed to do was call a shout out to the dining room, asking for volunteers. I learned that a sink full of dirty dishes is of less importance to the Lord than a heart full of bitterness and self-righteousness.

Personal Application

Here are four tips to stop passive-aggressive behaviour.

1. Acknowledge the fruits of such behaviour are not beneficial in the long run. Take a good look at your relationships. Do you have a sense that your friends are just putting up with you?

2. Ask honest questions of others. Don't assume that what you consider to be of great importance is of great importance to them. Make your needs known. In my example, I should have asked if anyone felt they could tear themselves away from the casual conversation to help me clear the table and serve dessert. If they had said no, I would have moved on to point three.

3. Share your perspective while acknowledging theirs. "It makes my heart glad that you are enjoying yourselves. However, I do need help to clear the table so I can serve dessert." If no one offered to help, I would have moved on to step four.

4. Make a firm request supported by logic. "Since there is no room left on the table, I won't be able to serve dessert. Please help me take care of the dishes" Clearly stating your request and your expectations without nagging or manipulation increases the likelihood that the person will comply.

5. Follow through. Using my example, by the lack of my friend's response to my request, I would presume their conversation was of more importance to them than meeting my need. I'd grab a cup of tea and let my guests enjoy their evening while I did the dishes. I would take the disappointment I felt to the Lord. I probably would not host a potluck again unless that potluck consisted of take out that was served on disposable dishware.

Bullies in the Sanctuary?

Zechariah 13:6 – And if one asks him, "What are these wounds on your back?" he will say, "The wounds I received in the house of my friends."

As I was the target of many schoolyard bullies; I became an expert on their tactics. I did my best to stay clear of the traps they laid before me. It was hard to avoid the obstacles they placed behind me. When I would inevitably fall, their taunts echoed in my ears long after my bruises faded. "Klutz! She can't even walk and chew gum at the same time; she's such a moron." Bullies knew how to push my emotional buttons and poked and prodded until I eventually lashed out in anger or I ran away in tears. "Wacko! Wimp, Crybaby!"

While crude, their methods were effective. The weak and the social outcasts were not welcome in a bully's world. Many of these young ruffians refined their tactics as they grew; adding social shunning, rumours, and psychological warfare to their arsenal.

I stumbled across the most infamous bully of my elementary schoolyard when we were in our twenties. I was hired as a temporary clerk in the vehicle leasing firm where he worked as a highly successful collections officer. He had grown into a muscle-bound man. Although he polished his bullying techniques to stay within the law, he continued to intimidate his victims through speech and body language.

Perhaps my childhood experiences heightened my awareness of subtle adult bullying within the Church. However, I have witnessed such harassment take place in just about every church I have attended. The old 'push and shove' technique is one such technique that I often see in play.

A person feels threatened or irritated by the behaviour, appearance, or social status of another believer. Perhaps their target is more attractive than they are. Perhaps their target's ministry is recognised by others, and theirs is not. Perhaps that person has spiritual giftings that the bully covets. Sometimes the target is socially inept and has the embarrassing habit of asking questions the bully isn't ready to answer. Maybe the target is on the outskirts of society. Perhaps their expression of worship challenges the status quo. Whatever the reason, they are perceived as a threat by the bully and must be removed.

Christian bullies cloak their passive aggressive attacks with civil niceties, pushing their victims to the breaking point. Through disconcerting stares, turned up noses, and whispered gossip, they effectively place their targets at their wit's end. By pointing out flaws and minimising strengths, these bullies push their victims toward frustration and hopelessness. By flaunting personal freedom in areas where their victims struggle; their targets despair that they will ever overcome their weaknesses. When their victims finally break and stumble under the immense pressure, bullies smugly justify their actions with judgmental statements. "See, he's just a backslider, good thing God exposed him before he hurt someone. I doubt he ever was a Christian."

Many a bully's victims have left the Church because of such behaviour. Both Jesus and Paul gave stern warnings to those who would cause someone to fall. While each person is responsible for their own sin, woe to those who purposefully drive someone to sin!

What is the antidote? How can we prevent Christian bullying? The Bible gives us clear instructions:

Romans 14:13 — "Let us not pass judgment on one another any longer, but rather decide never to put a stumbling-block or hindrance in the way of a brother."

Galatians 5:13 — "For You were called to freedom, brothers. Only do not use your freedom as an opportunity for the flesh, but through love serve one another."

Ephesians 4:29 — "Let no corrupting talk come out of your mouths, but only such as is good for building up, as fits the occasion, that it may give grace to those who hear."

Father God, we repent of hiding our insecurities by focusing our attention on the weaknesses of others. Give us the courage to approach those we have caused to stumble so we may humbly ask for forgiveness. Bring back the prodigals that we helped to create for we are helpless to bring them back ourselves. Holy Spirit, guard our tongues and our hearts. When we are fearful of others because they are different from us, remind us that we have nothing to fear. You are our protector. When we are envious of their talents and ministries, reassure us. Remind us of this truth: there is always enough of Your love. It will never run out.

Personal Application

If you recognise yourself as a bully through the descriptions listed above, get help. Most bullies were either bullied themselves or grew up in dysfunctional homes. Clean up your messes; repent of your past behaviours.

Just a few years ago, a bully from my childhood searched for me through Social Media. He sincerely apologised for his behaviour. I forgave him and found healing through our brief interaction. You can be an agent of healing!

If you recognise a bully culture in your church or fellowship, speak out. Confront in love when necessary. If you are in leadership, meet with your team and set a firm anti-bullying mandate and openly express that mandate to those you serve. Establish a victim-friendly protocol that opens the door to those under you to bring their concerns.

KISSED BY A GAVEL?

Some people are highly suspicious of anyone who appears to be consistently happy, loving, kind, or successful. However, they might not think themselves to be suspicious by nature. They probably consider themselves to be wise and discerning.

There are organisations who proclaim they have a divine mandate to hold court against other ministries. Their followers are people who consider themselves to be just as wise and discerning as the organisation. These groups create websites, podcasts, and conferences with the intention of exposing the faults of ministries and people who don't meet their doctrinal standards. When they receive an invitation to engage in a dialogue with those they accuse, they usually decline. Their reasoning? They won't allow themselves to be defiled by heresy. Sound familiar? In Jesus' day, those folks belonged to the Scribes and Pharisees.

Some people believe they have been gifted the unique ability to hold those around them to the highest of standards while maintaining unconditional love. These self-appointed accountability partners make sure their partnerships are one-sided. They usually aren't receptive when lovingly confronted about flaws in their own lives.

Not Always All Together

They proclaim they love all humanity. However, these folks usually reserve unconditional love for those they meet in passing. It's easy to love the homeless guy they walk past every day on their way to work. It's easy to forgive the person who closes the elevator door in their face. It's easy not to judge the anonymous girl who confesses a sexual addiction to them in a ministry line at church.

Although they love perfect strangers perfectly, they set impossibly high standards for those in their immediate circles. Their love holds hidden conditions that quickly become apparent to others when they fail to meet conditions secretly laid down. Relatively healthy people distance themselves from those who exhibit such behaviour. They know it is impossible to respond to such high standards. They also know by attempting to meet those standards, they are enabling a perfectionist spirit. When the relatively healthy do step away from such dysfunction, they are accused of being self-righteous and exclusive.

Those who set such high standards are known to ambush their loved ones by dragging them into a kangaroo court where they appoint themselves as judge, jury, and prosecution. Although they use non-judgmental Christian clichés in their carefully worded charges, they reached their verdict long before the defendant is called to respond to the accusations brought forth against them.

Heaven help the accused if they dare ask for a brief recess to collect their thoughts and heaven help the accused if they dare refute any of the charges laid against them! The guilty are sentenced to a prolonged "time out" with no set release date. The condemned have no idea if or when they will receive parole. They walk away feeling as if they've been kissed by a gavel.

Authentic love does not punish by withholding love. It does not ostracise. It loves first and confronts second. It presumes the best about a person; it is slow to believe the worst. Humility is its foundation.

_____

Personal Application

James 1:19 – "Know this, my beloved brothers: let every person be quick to hear, slow to speak, slow to anger."

Luke 6:31 – "And as you wish that others would do to you, do so to them."

I find that I slip into judgmental behaviour and attitudes when I am feeling insecure or when I am carrying internal shame or guilt, real or imagined. Do you carry a deep-seated burden of unworthiness? God is crazy about you. He loves you and isn't just putting up with you. You didn't slip through the cracks in disguise, wrapped in the Robes of Righteousness. The robes He gave you are transparent, and He sees you for who you are, and loves you for who you are. Let that truth seep in. If you have a heart understanding of His great love for you and His unfathomable grace extended toward you, you will have a hard time judging another person. After all, He sees them through the same lens He sees you.

Not Always All Together

SWEET OR SOUR?

Picture, if you will, identical metal barrels standing side by side on a wooden pallet. The barrels were exposed to the same atmosphere, humidity and temperature. A scientist stands behind safety glass in an adjoining room and presses a button that sets a machine into motion. Two barrels are randomly selected, and each receives an identical hard blow. The force knocks both barrels over, and they land on the edge of the pallet, causing their contents to slowly seep out.

Acid spills from the first barrel onto the wooden pallet, burning a hole through the wood and sending a sickeningly sour odour through the air. However, a lightly scented sweet oil drips down from the second barrel onto the pallet, its subtle scent eventually overcoming the sour stench, and the oil's sheen adds a rich lustre to the wood.

Adversity exposes our inner character by removing the facades we put in place to mask our character flaws and insecurities. When you face misfortune, persecution or crisis, what pours out? The acid of bitterness stored up from unforgiven offences or the sweet fragrance of a heart surrendered to Christ?

Personal Application

It's never too late to ask the Master to create in you a clean heart. (Psalm 51:10) Through God's grace, you can be a carrier of His healing and encouragement, even when life knocks you down.

Take some time today and meditate on the following scripture and quote. Humbly ask the Lord for help, ask for His forgiveness, and accept that forgiveness. Then take it one step further by genuinely apologising to those you have harmed by your words.

Luke 6:45 — "The good person out of the good treasure of his heart produces good, and the evil person out of his evil treasure produces evil, for out of the abundance of the heart his mouth speaks."

"Guard your tongue, and use it for good instead of evil. How many marriages or friendships have been destroyed because of criticism that spiraled out of control? How many relationships have broken down because of a word spoken thoughtlessly or in anger? A harsh word can't be taken back; no apology can fully repair its damage."
Billy Graham

Psst, Heard Any Good Gossip Lately?

Psst! Heard any good gossip lately? No, I'm not talking about that juicy tidbit of gossip that tastes good when first swallowed but curdles in one's spirit as soon as it is digested. I'm not talking about the type of news that makes you rub your hands together in glee because you just knew the 'truth' would come out. No, destructive, manipulative, vindictive, and secretive gossip is never productive. Enough scriptures warn us to keep away from this sort of speech, I won't go into them here. We are cautioned to stay away from evildoers who delight in the downfall of others.

So then, what type of gossip am I talking about? Is there such a thing as 'good' gossip? I firmly believe the answer is yes! Can you encourage and bless others by speaking behind their backs? I resoundingly say, Yes and Amen! Is there gossip that spurs us on to good works? Yes! Not only does it spur us on to good works, but it also speaks new life, creates new dreams, and brings forth blessings.

Have you ever passed by a group of people and heard your name mentioned in a positive light? Have you ever met someone for the first time, only for him or her to say, "Oh, I've heard such good things about you!" Have you ever felt that rush of happiness when someone notices you in a room and waves you over, exclaiming, "We were just talking about you!" By the expressions on the faces of everyone involved with the conversation, you can tell they were speaking well of you. Have you felt that deep sense of relief and gratitude when you heard that a friend defended your character in your absence? That is the type of good gossip I am talking about! It tastes good on the tongue and feels even better in your spirit.

What's the point? *"Do unto others as you would have others do unto you!"* (Luke 6:31) If you want to be blessed, bless others first. Let the words of your mouth be uplifting and encouraging. Be the first to look for the good in others and be the first to share that good with others.

Begin to look for the good, and you'll be surprised what good you will find. You'll even notice it in those people with whom you have not yet developed a heart connection. You'll discover traits that once bothered you in a person now are qualities you admire. What once looked like nit-picking perfectionism now resembles a heart that wants to give its best to God and others. Diligently hunt for the hidden treasure.

When people try to draw you into a group that is intent on malicious gossip, swallow any fear of man and speak the truth in love. Build a dyke of edification against the rising tides of maliciousness and pettiness that threaten to erode the works of God. Not only do you protect the gossip's target, but you hinder the meddlers from causing further damage. Lead by example, raising good points about the gossip's target. If the ungodly conversation continues, walk away. If a brother or sister has a grievance with another Christian and speaks maliciously about them in your presence, bring the following passage to your remembrance.

Matthew 18:15 — "If your brother sins against you, go and tell him his fault, between you and him alone. If he listens to you, you have gained your brother. But if he does not listen, take one or two others along with you, that every charge may be established by the evidence of two or three witnesses. If he refuses to listen to them, tell it to the church. And if he refuses to listen even to the church, let him be to you as a Gentile and a tax collector."

Shut your ears to prayer requests that are nothing more than thinly disguised rumours. Be the one person with whom your friends know they should not share gossip. Pray that others will follow your example.

With an attitude of love and humility, don't be afraid to ask others the following questions:

1. How do they know the validity of what they are sharing?
2. Have they attempted to reconcile with the person who offended them? Have they asked God for clarity?
3. If they are sharing second-hand information, why do they feel you need to know that information?

When you're tempted to bring charges against another believer, ask yourself the following questions:

1. Am I seeking vindication?
2. Am I trying to justify harbouring unforgiveness?
3. Am I attempting to preserve my right to be right?

4. Will I bring encouragement to the hearer of my words?

5. Does the hearer of my words need to know this information?

6. Would I say these things in the presence of the one of whom I am speaking?

Be the first to brag about those who have blessed you. Be the first to share the good news and be the first to point out those people who are a blessing to you and the body of Christ.

Yes, there is such a thing as good gossip. Earnestly seek the gift of encouragement.

Personal Application

Here are a few scriptures for further thought:

Psalm 37:30 — "The mouth of the righteous utters wisdom, and his tongue speaks justice."

Proverbs 31:8 — "Open your mouth for the mute, for the rights of all who are destitute."

1 Peter 4:10-11 — "As each has received a gift, use it to serve one another, as good stewards of God's varied grace: whoever speaks, as one who speaks oracles of God; whoever serves, as one who serves by the strength that God supplies—in order that in everything God may be glorified through Jesus Christ. To him belong glory and dominion forever and ever. Amen."

Ephesians 4:29 — "Let no corrupting talk come out of your mouths, but only such as is good for building up, as fits the occasion, that it may give grace to those who hear."

Not Always All Together

I'd Like to Get to Know Them, But...

I sighed as I watched a young husband and wife escort their four children into the sanctuary of our church. *Such a lovely family and obviously a successful one by the look of his suit.* With a rueful shake of my head, I continued my internal conversation. *Nice folk but apparently too good for me.* I was wearing faded jeans and a worn-out sweatshirt. Being a home missionary in a large urban centre didn't allow me the luxury of new clothes.

I kept my eye on this family over the months. As time went on, I learned of their passion for the poor and their advocacy for the disenfranchised. *Great,* I thought. *Not only do they look perfect, but they are in an entirely different league of Christianity than me. Look how worn her Bible is!*

As weeks progressed into months, my inner off-the-cuff judgments of this family built a self-constructed wall of intimidation. I had no idea that I had built that wall. I wasn't aware of the judgements I formed against this precious family. If anyone had asked me my opinion of this couple, I would have sung their praises even as I kept my distance.

One Sunday, I arrived a few minutes late to church, and the service was packed. An usher escorted me to the only seat available—at the end of the perfect family's pew. Swallowing my panic, I sat on the very edge of the crowded pew. As I bent to place my purse under our pew, my nose wrinkled. The tell-tale stench of stale tobacco wafted from a leather coat that I recognised as belonging to the perfect husband of this perfect family. Having grown up with smokers, I knew that that intense of an odour could only infuse the jacket of a habitual smoker. With that single whiff, my presumptions about this family fell away.

Silently, I repented and renounced the wall I had built between myself and this family. Although I would never condone smoking, God used this brother's struggle with cigarettes to teach me a lesson. I judged this family by their appearance and outer behaviour alone. By the way, smoking is no longer a snare for this couple; they quit the habit a few weeks after I sat in their pew.

I am grateful for God's intervention as I now consider this couple to be my family. We have wept together, laughed together, and shared many meals together. They embraced me in their hearts. I let them past my walls. They continue to stand beside me in times of crisis, and they rely on my prayers when their family faces crises of its own.

I have heard many sermons warning against judging the poor and homeless. However, I have heard few sermons warning against judging the successful and the apparently put-together.

Joy Dawson once told the story of an incredibly wealthy woman. She confided to Joy that she was terribly lonely. This godly friend gave generously to missions and sponsored philanthropic endeavours across the globe. Those whom she would have loved to know better kept their distance. They feared that an offer of friendship would be seen by her as a means to get to her money. Then there were those who saw her as nothing more than a potential supporter of their cause.

Personal Application

Proverbs 25:8 (MSG) — "Don't jump to conclusions — there may be a perfectly good explanation for what you just saw."

Do you make assumptions about those who appear to have their act together? Do you judge someone because they happen to drive a nice car or live in a big house? Do you assume they spend most of their money on themselves?

Judge not the one who apparently has it all together; judge not the poor. Judge not the perfect mother; judge not the frazzled one. Judge not the guy with the nice car; judge not the guy with the old beater. Simply put, judge not.

Not Always All Together

YOU CAN MAKE A DIFFERENCE

Never view your sphere of influence as being too small to make much of a difference in the grand scheme of life. Unless you grew up as a recluse, locked away in a darkened room, never once leaving your home, you would have brushed against thousands of lives by the time your life on earth ended.

Daily routines offer opportunities to carry God's hope, healing, and restoration in your world. Fostering a relationship with a favourite cashier at the local grocery store could lead to an opportunity to pray with her when you sense she's having a rough day. God might want to use you to bless the guy behind the counter at your gas station with a thank you note accompanied by a gift card to the coffee shop across the street. Unbeknownst to you, the customer right before you chewed him out for an insignificant slip-up. That seemingly disinterested university student who catches the bus with you every morning might be severely depressed.

Perhaps the one God leads you to is a member of your family. Keep alert and don't allow familiarity with a loved one to dull your senses to Holy Spirit's promptings. Don't take your loved ones for granted. Sometimes, the routine tasks of our day distract us from seeing their hearts. Ask Holy

Spirit for His perspective as you pray for your children, your spouse, and your extended family.

If you are single, ask the Lord to highlight friends who need an encouraging word or a listening ear. If you are housebound and live alone, you can touch lives through email and Social Media. Better yet, pick up the phone.

Mother Teresa encouraged those who hoped to follow her footsteps. *"Never worry about numbers. Help one person at a time and always start with the person nearest you."*

Heidi Baker, who has touched thousands upon thousands of lives in Africa and beyond, simplified it even further. *"Stop for the one."*

Personal Application

If you feel insignificant, study the lives of David, Saul, and Gideon. All these men came from humble beginnings. David and Gideon chose to take God at His word and stepped out in obedience, trusting His favour. Saul never overcame his insecurities. Those insecurities grew into paranoia, and resulted in his destruction.

List five times that you made a positive difference in someone's life, no matter how small you judge that difference to be. If you can't think of five instances, ask someone to remind you.

A BAND OF SISTERS

A few years ago, I met with a group of Christian singles one Easter Saturday for dinner. Most of us didn't have family nearby, and many of us would have spent the entire weekend alone, if not for this little get-together. We feasted on friendship just as much as we feasted on roast beef and all the trimmings. After we tidied the kitchen and divvied up the leftovers amongst the bachelors, we drifted into the living room.

There came a moment where we shifted into quiet contentment. Worship music that had been playing softly in the background now became our focus. The presence of the Lord was palpable, sweet and gentle. Spontaneous prayer and worship erupted. When I next looked at the clock, it was 4:30 AM. We had been in prayer for over six hours.

Despite the late hour, I was reluctant to go home. Two of my friends echoed my sentiment. We wanted more. With much expectancy, we decided to watch the sunrise together and found a vantage point that overlooked our city. At first light, we opened our car windows and cranked up the worship music. My friends couldn't contain their joy. They danced on top of that hill as we sang the words, "*Praise to the One who gave us His Son.*" I could barely sing as waves of joy crashed over me.

We were a small group of women, much like the group that made their way to Jesus' tomb. They brought with them an offering of spices to anoint His body. It was all they could do in return for all Jesus had done for them. Their Master brought freedom to their lives, healed their loved ones, and whispered hope into their hearts. Little did they know that a great reward was waiting for them at the tomb. Because of their willingness to serve Jesus for what they presumed was one last time, those women were the first to hear the joyous news. *"Why do you look for the living among the dead? He is not here; he has risen!"* (Luke 24:5-6)

Personal Application

"Whatever troubles are weighing you down are not chains. They are featherweight when compared to the glory yet to come. With a sweep of a prayer and the praise of a child's heart, God can strip away any cobweb." - Joni Eareckson Tada, *Diamonds in the Dust*. (London: Marshall Pickering, 1993)

The band of women that made their way up to Jesus' tomb were deeply grieved, and yet, that grief didn't stop them from giving sacrificially. Their sacrifice was met with a kiss of Glory. Take a moment to praise God for who He is and what He has done for you, even in the midst of personal hardship. Don't rush from that place, stay long enough to hear His response.

LEARN YOUR LESSONS WELL

As a child, I often tagged behind my mother as she did chores around the house. I liked to match socks for her, and it was fun to collect the pegs as she removed items from the clothes line. As those were the days before fabric softeners, I watched as my mother fluffed each towel with a vigorous shake. Although I use a dryer and fabric softening wool balls now, I still vigorously shake my towels before I fold them. That is the way I learned!

As an adult, I find that I still learn best by following an example. I do better by seeing than just by reading. For example, I learned more about cultivating a servant-heart from observing experts than by listening to sermons or reading books on the subject.

While on a two-month outreach in Colombia, South America, I worked with local Christians. They didn't speak much English, and my Spanish was limited. It was my first cross-cultural experience. Although these brothers and sisters in Christ had little, they gave generously. An ice-cold health drink appeared in my hand when I struggled with the heat. They took their showers last, despite the protests of our team, ignoring our insistence that we use a rotation schedule. No matter how frugal our team was with the hot water, by the time the Colombians showered, the water was icy cold. A child's comb was left on my pillow as a small token of remembrance from a Colombian national who prayed faithfully for our team. I treasured that comb for years. I was one of her special prayer targets, and I was grateful for her prayers of protection over me.

A few weeks before this outreach, I spent Christmas in a remote northern Ontario settlement with a missionary family. When one of my classmates heard that I had no place to go during our winter break, she insisted that I spend Christmas with her family. I was hesitant, as I knew her father was fighting cancer.

Many families would have closed ranks as they dealt with such a life-threatening health crisis. This precious family opened their home and selflessly gave of their valuable time with their dad. I was greeted with hugs and gracious hospitality.

The family's lifestyle was traditional, and their church culture valued simplicity. Although I was a city girl through and through, they welcomed me in. I was considered one of their daughters that week. I learned what family devotions were all about by sitting at their kitchen table as their cancer-ridden father read from the Bible every evening.

Much to my amazement, there were home-made gifts under the tree for me on Christmas morning; a pair of slippers in my favourite colour, along with a crocheted bookmark. My friend's mother stayed up late several nights to knit those slippers for me, as my stay with them was a last-minute visit.

I learned much from a tiny comb, an ice-cold bottle of soda, a warm shower, a pair of slippers and a bookmark. All priceless gifts. Sacrificial giving often has little monetary value, and yet the fruits of such giving are eternal.

Personal Application

"Preach the Gospel at all times. When necessary, use words." - Francis of Assisi

Like it or not, we are all teachers by the example we set as we go about our daily lives. Your children learn how to respond to stress by watching you respond to stress. Your employees learn how to deal with difficult clients by the way you deal with difficult customers. Your non-Christian friends quietly observe how you respond to poor service at your favourite hangout.

Look for opportunities to bless others and then do so, with little fanfare. Through your example, you will inspire others to do likewise, even if they are not always all together!

Not Always All Together

ABOUT THE AUTHOR

Hello, I'm Katherine. I am a Christian, and my life is found in Christ, and so His name is sprinkled throughout the pages of this book. I live with a neurological disorder called Charcot Marie Tooth Disease, but my disability does not hinder me from living an active, productive life. I worked with Youth With A Mission for 13 years, eventually resettling in Alberta, Canada. However, my disability progressed to the point where I was no longer able to work in a regular work environment. After consulting with my doctors and after seeking the advice of trusted pastors and family members, I decided to hang up the traditional work hat, and I now live on a small disability pension.

Someone once said, "You can take the minister out of the pulpit but you can't take the ministry out of the minister." I continue to minister around the world without taking a step from my apartment through the Internet. I Lift My Eyes Ministries, now known as Katherine Walden Ministries, was founded in 1996 and reaches thousands on a daily basis, reaching more people than I would have ever imagined when I was involved in missions! I continue to encourage and inspire fellow '*not always all together*' brothers and sisters in Christ through my writings and one-on-one mentoring. I am actively involved with my local church, and have served as both a small group leader and facilitator over the years.

You can find me on Facebook and Twitter, as well as my website, katherinewalden.com. On occasion, you'll find me pop up on Instagram and YouTube as well.

Acknowledgements

Thank you to my incredible team of international proofreaders: Alice Briggs, Pam Lacey, Aaron Reini, Jane Pietroniro, Priscilla Li, John Spencer, Grace Hauer, and Roxann Miller. Together, you helped the *not-all-together me* put together a book that I hope blesses many. Thank you to all the rest of my closet Grammar Police friends for your valuable input.

Once again, I must extend special thanks to Alice Briggs of alicearlene.com for lending her amazing artistic talents, graphic art skills, and spiritual sensibilities to this project.

Special thanks to my video crew, Charlene Dyer and Jane Pietroniro. Although we couldn't use the footage due to technical issues, your selfless kindness in the midst of a heatwave is forever remembered.

Back Cover Photo Credit: Blair Bisson, Edmonton Alberta

Words cannot express my deep gratitude for the love, wisdom, encouragement, exhortation, and affirmation I have received through the Body of Christ, both locally and internationally. Without my band of relentless cheerleaders, this book would not have been completed.

Not Always All Together

FURTHER RESOURCES

Find Katherine's books on Amazon and Kindle:

Seasons: Reflections on Changes Throughout Life

A compilation of 90 inspirational devotions and thought-provoking writings, penned with humour, wisdom and compassion. Through powerful imagery that is often allegorical, this devotional will motivate you to consider a delightful myriad of uplifting possibilities and inspire you to press on, no matter what season of life you are presently experiencing.

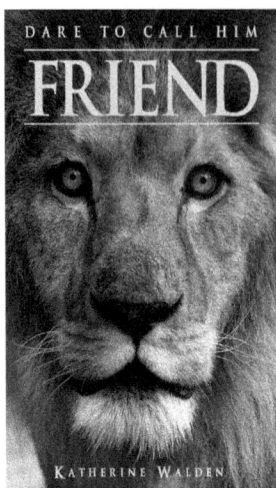

Dare to Call Him Friend

Not only does God call you friend, He also invites you into His inner circle. Yes, there is a risk involved if you accept that invitation. He'll lead you out of your comfort zone. He'll turn your life inside out and upside down. The risk is worth it! Another great devotional by Katherine, full of insights drawn from her experiences on the mission field and the home front.

Weekly Email:

Sign up for Katherine's weekly email list and receive a devotional as well as seven inspirational Christian quotes from Katherine's vast library of inspiring and thought provoking gems. Find out more at katherinewalden.com

Vlogs and Live Events:

Katherine regularly posts inspirational quotes and thoughts on

Facebook and Instagram, as well as on her YouTube channel. Look for the occasional Facebook Live as well!

Contact Katherine at contact@katherinewalden.com

www.ingramcontent.com/pod-product-compliance
Lightning Source LLC
Chambersburg PA
CBHW061732020426
42331CB00006B/1209